Praise for Business Blather

"Business Blather" is filled with practical examples that show the before and after of nonsensical prose that confound rather than clarify what we want to say. One can't help but laugh at the ridiculousness we are all guilty of when talking in business jargon. This book is a wonderful reminder of the impact of using simple, powerful language, whether it's in your emails, LinkedIn profile, or business mission."

—Ronni Burns, Professor of Communication, NYU Stern School of Business

"Business Blather is as educational as it is enjoyable. Very Jerry— cuts to the chase—easy to understand and ready-to-use tips to advance business communications."

—Ajay Srinivas, President and CEO, Cetalus LLC

"FYI – at the end of the day, in the fullness of time, when all is said and done – I can tell you that this very very nice book offers truly bountiful insights, really sage advice, and extremely helpful illustrations of how to say what you have to say in a real-world business environment. And if that sentence seems to make sense, you (and I) badly need the instruction provided by McTigue in Business Blather."

—Morris B. Holbrook, W. T. Dillard Professor of Marketing Emeritus, Graduate School of Business, Columbia University

Also by Jerry (G. Gaynor) McTigue

Life's Little Frustration Book
(St. Martin's Press)

More Life's Little Frustration Book
(St. Martin's Press)

You Know You're Middle Aged When...
(Penguin Books)

How Not to Make Love to a Woman
(Dove Books)

Why Make Yourself Crazy?
(Pick Me Up Books)

400 Ways to Stop Stress Now...and Forever!
(Pick Me Up Books)

Business Blather

STOP USING WORDS THAT SOUND GOOD BUT SAY NOTHING!

JERRY MCTIGUE

Pick Me Up Books™

Pick Me Up Books™

CONTENTS

PART TWO BETTER COMMUNICATION. IN ALL ITS FORMS.

LINKEDIN PROFILES 44

WEBSITES 55

PART THREE IF I'VE LEARNED ANYTHING...

PART ONE A FAILURE TO COMMUNICATE

1 This book needs no introduction

In truth, does *any* book need an introduction?

Introductions (a.k.a. prefaces, forewords, author's notes, et al.) have become halfhearted or longwinded affairs written out of habit or convention with the knowledge that many people, unfortunately, don't read them.

So why even write them?

First lesson of this book. If you have something to say come out and say it. Don't waste good words that may go unheeded or the reader's time with unnecessary previews or congratulatory acknowledgements yet to be earned.

Lose the lead-ins, buildups and drumrolls. Get right to the nub.

2 Which, in this case, is...

Business communication is abysmal.

In all its forms. Websites. Emails. Advertising. Presentations.

1

Letters. Reports. Interoffice correspondence. Articles. Resumes. LinkedIn profiles. Speeches. What did I miss?

It's overwrought. Redundant. Tedious. Unspecific. Self-interested. Presumptuous. Cryptic. Stilted. Unintelligible. *Maddening*. All combining to create a toothless lexicon some have dubbed "corporatese."

Or, as this book calls it, business blather.

Sure, not all business communication is awful. Not everyone is guilty. There's some great work being done out there. On many fronts. Brava! Bravo!

But the vast chunk of it? Blecchhh! Makes you want to gag. Because in reality, if you pay close attention to what you're reading, or hearing...*it says nothing*. Nothing new, nothing substantive, nothing thought-provoking, nothing clarifying, nothing exciting...nothing anyone hasn't written, or we haven't heard, a million times.

You would think, therefore, that its perpetrators would make an attempt to improve it. That they would note the glazed looks and early onset napping their work engenders and say something fresh, engaging, incisive.

You would think. But there's one underlying problem, one huge overriding obstacle that prevents this from happening.

It sounds good.

Oh yeah, it *sounds* good. Exactly how the purveyors of this pretentious jibber-jabber think it's supposed to sound. Or believe it's obligated to sound. A style of communication (or dearth of it) so ingrained in our business culture it's dominated the discourse for decades. An obeisance to the corporate gods that's become almost cultish.

Never mind we readers and listeners have little idea what they're babbling about. We're made to feel that if we don't understand what's being set forth *it's our fault*. That we should be so taken with the ostentatious, rhetorical flourishes of the verbiage, the acronyms, buzzwords and smug jargon, we'll be impelled to further explore, or take action upon, what it's trying to convey.

Fatal mistake. In this nanosecond attention span world, even the slightest obfuscation of language is grounds for immediate dismissal of subject matter.

3 So give us an example, will ya?

Happy to. To help you get the drift of what I'm carping about, here's an actual excerpt from a company attempting to explain its mission:

> BUSINESS BLATHER: We see the essence of our work as a virtuous circle of insight, impact, and trust. We

continually strive to generate deep insight into what drives value creation and competitive advantage in our clients' businesses and the economy as a whole. We work closely with clients to convert insights into strategies, whose implementation will have a substantial positive impact on performance. Consistently delivering impact earns the trust that is the foundation of lasting relationships. These relationships serve as a platform for still deeper insights and more significant impact."

Seriously?

Now, you may think this sounds just fine. And with a few mental contortions, may even extract some useful meaning out of the loops of lofty terms and vague concepts.

But consider. In the 88 words you've just been waltzed through, is there any inkling what kind of business this company is engaged in? What their primary product or service is? How they whomp their competition? Most importantly, what specific benefits you can expect to gain?

Rather, in an effort to come off as an altruistic, all-empowered corporate Mother Theresa, which defies credulity, they totally blow a perfect opportunity to differentiate themselves.

Why make a statement so generic and lacking in particulars, virtually any type of business, from a one-person consultancy to a multinational conglomerate, could make the same chest-puffing boasts?

In fact, *many have.* If you put quotes around the sentence *"We continually strive to generate deep insight into what drives value creation and competitive advantage in our clients' businesses and the economy as a whole."* and google it, you'll find several entities using these exact words! (An impossible coincidence.)

So much for unique selling proposition. So much for individuality.

The addiction to corporate blather is so strong, otherwise successful companies will glom on to its grandiose declarations rather than make a distinct and honest pitch to its audience. And suffer an identity deficit for their trouble. Business communication is almost becoming an oxymoron.

Now, compare that mission statement to this one:

> **BETTER: DroneVideos.com was created to provide uniform excellence in aerial photography by establishing the first and largest nationwide network of highly qualified drone operators who are fully vetted, licensed and insured. Most importantly, they exhibit exceptional skills and artistry in shooting beautifully composed Ultra HD footage. Our CEO manually reviews each project to ensure it is 100% perfect and worthy of our name and reputation.**

Eureka. No question which of the two statements leaves you with a solid grasp of what the company is about and how you can benefit from it.

Which is exactly what this book is about. In this first part, you'll learn how to break free from the stranglehold of mystifying corporatese and start writing and speaking in clear, concise, engaging language, whatever the medium.

In Part Two, I show you how to apply these concepts to specific forms of business communication, whether you're advertising products and services, corresponding with associates, giving a presentation, applying for a job, creating a website, launching an email campaign, publishing a white paper, composing a press release...it's all covered.

Finally, in Part Three I offer some hard-won wisdom gleaned over my writing career that has consistently held true, regardless of what trends, philosophies and transitions have come and gone.

4 So who are *you*, telling *me*, how to communicate?

Thought you'd ask. As a professional writer—copywriter, journalist, author, scriptwriter—I've spent more years than I care to admit crafting virtually every kind of business communication imaginable. *Times a thousand.*

I've created advertising for countless clients in myriad industries, from top global brands to tiny startups; written articles and essays for national magazines and major city newspapers; scripted numerous promotional videos, PowerPoint and audio/visual presentations; penned all manner of websites, email campaigns, blog posts, press releases, brochures, proposals, TV and radio commercials, speeches, white papers, direct mail, you name it; and managed to squeeze in seven books (including this one).

As they say, I know a thing or two because...well, you know the rest. And a lot of what I see today is atrocious, a world of opportunity lost to an almost religious adherence to an ineffectual style of communication that, to repeat, sounds good but says nothing.

I wrote this book from the heart. Actually, spleen might be a better body part to describe it. Regardless, it would be an understatement to say it is a work of passion.

Full disclosure: when I started out I was proudly spewing out the very drivel I decry today. What did I know?

But it didn't take long to realize that if you're serving up the same hash in the same affected way everyone else is, how could it possibly stand out and do the job it's supposed to? It wasn't fun either, not what I signed on to.

So early on I vowed: if you're going to take the time to sit down and write something, maybe even forge a career out of it, make the extra effort to express yourself in a way that isn't a cure for insomnia. You might even grow to love the process.

I did. Now it's your turn. Let's get started.

(One more disclosure: that DroneVideos.com mission statement was written by me.)

5 You are what you eat...*and write*

Business blather is a lot like junk food.

Eating sugary, fatty, salty, processed stuff not only lacks essential nutrients needed for good health, it fills you up so you're less likely to consume more nutritious fare.

In the same way, while blather may "taste" (sound) good, it isn't really nourishing your understanding of what it's addressing.

Further, it's stealing time and attention you might spend consuming more useful information. Lose-lose.

Here's an example:

> BUSINESS BLATHER: We are a full-service accounting firm that caters to your specific business needs. As a team of

highly trained professionals, we provide targeted accounting services tailored to the ever-changing needs of your growing business. With a collective 60 years of experience, we are equipped to assist you in every capacity. Our passion is to work with business owners to create a unique accounting program that focuses on your business's financial goals.

You might think that sounds pretty decent, right? You get a general idea of what they do.

So what's my problem?

This: The passage subscribes to the notion that if you have little to say, say it again. And again. Okay, we get it. You serve your clients' needs. Then repeat that almost verbatim. And for good measure throw in "goals," another way of saying needs.

Would it have killed the writer to mention what some of those "specific business needs" might be? And give an example or two of what "targeted accounting services" they offer that meet those needs? Or capacities they're "equipped to assist you" with?

Hey, give 'em a chance, you protest. They'll get to it. Trouble is, the reader may never get to it. The average visitor spends less than 15 seconds on a website. This is probably why. You've wasted precious seconds of their time spouting vague redundancies.

Don't make people fish around for the information they came for. Put it right out there, upfront, so they're compelled to read more.

> BETTER: Overwhelmed by the complexities of payroll? We unravel it for you. Books in disarray? We're masters of today's most efficient accounting systems. Crushed by taxes? We'll help you slash them. We're a full-service accounting firm our clients love because they don't have to deal with this stuff. While saving a bundle. Learn more.

In just 53 words this candid introduction blows away the 71-word pre-ramble it follows. It hits the prospect's pain points. Offers answers. And presents a call to action urging readers to explore further, a critical element the first statement lacks.

The takeaway? Say something that immediately whets the reader's appetite, offers specific benefits they can sink their teeth into, invites them to learn more. Avoid needless repetition, superfluous words and generalities, the junk food of communications.

> TIP: What's with this gimmick of describing experience in dog years? 60 years of collective experience means nothing if you don't know how many people work there. It could be 60 novices with a year each. Or one old relic with 59 years and an assistant with one. Or anything in between. Avoid see-through arguments readers or listeners can easily deconstruct.

6 Sound-good, say-nothing expressions

In business, boy do they sling the lingo, crank out slick buzzwords with little purpose other than to swagger or ascribe to mundane topics far more significance than they merit.

Rather than win advocates, affected language leaves target audiences confused, intimidated, annoyed.

How often does something you read or hear fly right over your head, make you feel inadequate or excluded when all you seek is simple understanding?

Stringing together arcane word sequences has become a kind of perverse art form. Take for example:

BUSINESS BLATHER: We recontextualized our product iterations to address postnatal parental needs.

What are we supposed to divine from that? C'mon, man, come out with it:

BETTER: We're launching a new line of baby products! Including innovative disposable diapers, wet wipes and rash protection.

Another:

BUSINESS BLATHER: With our collective interdepartmental

functionality, we possess the bandwidth to offer businesses the insurance modalities and feature sets you seek.

Uh, yeah, but what exactly are you hiding behind that curtain of ambiguity?

BETTER: We're fully equipped to offer an array of feature-rich commercial insurance products, including Group Life, Medical, Workers' Comp, Business Interruption, Liability, and more.

As you'll note in the above examples, citing specific items crushes vague characterizations of them. Why withhold or delay critical information? Who's got time for that?

Or, why tippy-toe around an issue like this interoffice email does:

BUSINESS BLATHER: Jason, I think this proposal needs more granularity in your delineation of our service tiers. You might also consider an amplification of what our differentiators are.

Hey Jason, *it's not you*. Anyone would do a double-take on that one. Your boss could just as easily have said:

BETTER: Jason: less theorizing, more detail please. Leave no one guessing what we offer, why we're better.

Dancing around your subject instead of simply making your point is anathema to a warp-speed world.

7 Draw them a picture

Here's a simple rule to guide your writing. If they can't visualize it, they probably won't get it.

When you use weirdly conjoined words that defy imagining, they serve only to produce contorted facial expressions.

Some examples, followed by ways these elusive concepts can be visualized by including the end results they refer to:

BUSINESS BLATHER: We collaboratively synthesized real-time systems.

BETTER: We merged real-time systems to create a financial data-on-demand center.

BUSINESS BLATHER: You can leverage our interoperable action items.

BETTER: You can share our telecommunication tips worldwide.

BUSINESS BLATHER: We productized tested aggregations.

BETTER: Our discoveries led to a new line of fertilizers.

Take-away: to enlighten rather than confound, avoid abstract wording in favor of characterizations the mind's eye can see.

Use vivid descriptions, metaphors and analogies in your writing that imprint not-easily-forgotten pictures on the brain. Like:

"your express elevator to sky-high sales"

"audio that rivals the London Philharmonic"

"the most explosive thing from China since fireworks"

Esoteric terminology is rampant in the corporate world. If its purveyors can't level with people, maybe what they're peddling isn't as good as they think it sounds.

8 Enough with the platitudes already

At the other end of the blather spectrum are litanies of clichés and banalities writers believe exude a corporate luster simply because virtually every corporation exudes them.

Not a good reason to lard your work with unedifying puffery, the communications equivalent of processed foods with zero fiber.

It has no staying power for a simple reason:

You are not something simply because you say you are.

Prove it. Illustrate it. Support it.

Unverified off-the-shelf pronouncements are innumerable—as many bloated corporate documents attest to.

Here is a compendium of some of the more common platitudes a company might gush:

> **BUSINESS BLATHER:** Our products are in a class by themselves. They adhere to the most exacting standards. Our customer service is second to none. We become your partner, treating your business as if it were our own.

Let's break these down, and why each is a loser.

> **BUSINESS BLATHER:** Our products are in a class by themselves.

Is that so? What products? What class?

> **BETTER:** We offer the only electric mowers with mulching, rear collection and side discharge options.

That's more like it. Put it right out there, up top. Then there's:

> **BUSINESS BLATHER:** We adhere to the most exacting standards.

Whose standards? Yours? Ed's? The lady down the street's?

> **BETTER:** All of our precision components comply with ISO 9001:2015 quality management system requirements.

Even if the reader doesn't know exactly what that is, validation from a respected source is way more convincing than none at all.

BUSINESS BLATHER: Our customer service is second to none.

True or not (mostly not), every company makes this claim in one form or another. To preempt the snickering, show proof:

BETTER: We won the Middlebury Merchants Association Customer Service Award five straight years.

This BS promise is also everywhere:

BUSINESS BLATHER: We become your partner, treating your business as if it were our own.

Really? You want to be my partner? Great. Cosign my business loans. Share in my losses. Help pay my taxes.

BETTER: We assign to you a team of experts, dedicated to achieving your sales and marketing objectives.

You get the idea. Replace those threadbare boasts with real substance, solid evidence, credible endorsements.

9 Break the padding and piling-on habit

The quote "I would have written a shorter letter, but I did not have the time" is attributed to the French mathematician Blaise Pascal back in 1657.

Yes, even 360+ years ago time was a valuable commodity. Pascal recognized this and understood that editing and brevity, hallmarks of good writing, require time. He apologized to his recipient for not taking enough of it, thus wasting theirs.

Today, when time is so precious it's measured in nanoseconds, and valued in dollars, let's not make the costly error of wasting our readers'—sending them on verbal scavenger hunts to figure out what in god's name we're talking about. Or worse, quickly losing their interest.

Not taking the time to write concisely isn't the only culprit needlessly lengthening our communications. It's the misguided notion, or insecurity, that more is better.

When you're being paid by your employer, client or audience for your insights and analysis, you may have a tendency to pad your emails, memos, reports, and presentations with useless filler to make it seem like they're getting their money's worth.

Once succumbing to that habit, there's no stopping you. Stretched-out sentences become bloated paragraphs, which become voluminous decks of mind-numbing prose. Or agonizingly lengthy speeches.

Warning. They're on to you. Today's information consumers like their whiskey neat. No watered-down meanderings. No hazy conceptualizing.

They don't appreciate being taken on a verbal joy ride. So indulge them with clear, crisp writing. Lots of meat, easy on the potatoes. Or incur their wrath.

Consider this excerpt:

> **BUSINESS BLATHER: Given today's challenges, many companies have turned to advanced information solutions to provide significantly more value to their customers and differentiate themselves in the commodity-based market. In order to continue to grow in this rapidly changing environment, these companies are proactively adapting to market conditions by examining and addressing each opportunity to improve operational efficiency and enhance their customers' buying experience.**

This passage is the poster child for suitably constructed, grammatically correct, they-sound-like-they-know-what-they're-talking-about...*gobbledygook.*

It strings together a series of vague concepts, never digging below the surface to give you a foothold of understanding through example or explanation what "challenges," "solutions," "value," "conditions," "opportunity," and "efficiency" they're alluding to.

Thus, rather than being informed, you're left to process a laundry list of indistinct ideas on your own—uncertain, unfulfilled.

Sure, you could argue this is the precursor to a more detailed discussion to follow (one I'd be inclined to pass on). But why subject readers to an incoherent prelude that serves only to flaunt the communicator's self-importance when they could easily have gone straight to the crux with something like this:

> BETTER: To keep pace with rapidly-changing consumer demands, companies are engaging on social media, mining digital data, and using advanced research techniques to bring the most wanted products to market faster, preempting their competition. To further profitability, they're applying powerful digital tools to improve production, distribution, marketing, and the customer experience.

Even if the reader doesn't read another word, you've given them real substance to chew on, things to relate to their own situation.

Which brings us to a critical inflection point in this book:

> Why in this era of shrinking attention spans even risk a paragraph laden with indeterminate statements that mystify more than illuminate?

If you want to break from (or never get started on) business blather, corporatese or whatever the heck you want to call it, you can begin right here.

Don't equivocate. Don't tease out your main points or package them in the verbal equivalent of Styrofoam peanuts. Be succinct, forthcoming, direct.

10 And another thing...

Shy away from pairings of words that add length but little or no incremental value, like in the above blather excerpt, "examining and addressing." Addressing, which by its nature would encompass examining, will do fine on its own, thank you.

Another frequent stretching-out tactic of business speak goes like this: "We sifted through, organized and analyzed the data..."

Unless you're trying to earn a merit badge, or are subtly complaining you're overworked, you just need to say "We analyzed the data." (You wouldn't say "I fetched, poured and ate a bowl of cereal.")

These pointless phrase extenders may seem like small change by themselves, but once you get hooked on them your text can expand like a Lycra® swimsuit. Imagine reading an entire white paper, report or dare I suggest book laden with such tedious excesses!

Tighten those sentences. Trim the fat. Get to the gist. Use an economy of words. And...

11 Explode out of the gate

I've always been a believer in great starts. Remember the movie *Raiders of the Lost Ark*? Rather than begin with the standard leisurely drive along a scenic highway, it introduces Indiana Jones in one of the most suspenseful and thrilling opening scenes in cinematic history. (I won't be a spoiler. Go watch.)

While our writing can't be this dramatic, your opening salvo, or lead as they call it in journalism, is critical. For a couple of reasons:

One, it's your first, and maybe only, chance to yank in your reader. So it better be good.

Two, it sets the tone and style for everything that follows. Important for the reader, important for *you*. Work hard on your beginning, be delighted with it. You'll gain the confidence to nail the rest of it.

Here are the opening paragraphs from two different business blogs on the importance of getting enough sleep. First:

> **BUSINESS BLATHER: We need to pay attention to the fundamentals of life: eating, sleeping and exercise. Taking a mindful approach to these pillars of well-being is more transformative than meditation alone.**

Say what? That opening could put *me* to sleep. First, it states the obvious, then follows with a puzzling reference to mindfulness and meditation that makes no sense (and I meditate). My interest isn't piqued. I'm not encouraged to read on.

> BETTER: "I'll sleep when I'm dead," said the frazzled entrepreneur to anyone who ventured to express concern. If this sounds like you, you're among more than a third of Americans who don't get enough sleep, according to the CDC.

Wow, that got my attention. First, a startling quote. Then, a disturbing statistic from a respected authority that struck home, leaving me to wonder if I'm among the sleep-deprived, enticing me to read further.

The first example starts with platitude, the second attitude. It might take longer to research and write a captivating opener, but you'll easily make up that time riding the momentum of an inspired kickoff.

Love your lead. It's the cornerstone of great writing.

12 Don't bury your lead

This irritates me no end. Maybe you, too. You're teased by a provocative title or headline into reading an article, blog post, website, ad, or email.

But the writer decides not to pay off that tantalizing come-on—like, "Experts Say 4-Second Workout All You Need"—anytime soon, stringing you along with useless leadups until they're good and ready to reveal what those elusive four seconds entail.

These kind of tactics used to work before internet clickbait artists made cynics of us all by flooding the web with enticing hooks that I, at least, no longer swallow.

If you fear you have to bury your lead because your material beyond the title is thin, maybe it isn't worth writing about.

You either need to shorten your piece or do a little more digging to come up with good usable substance to support your premise.

More publications seem to be getting the message that delayed payoffs may be hurting readership, even going so far as to start with a bulleted summary of what the full article covers.

I love that approach, as it accommodates those with limited time, while presenting inducements for others to read the whole piece.

Skip the elaborate buildups that tick people off. Go right to the sweet spot.

13 Overwrought means underthought

Why does virtually everything written or uttered today have to be embellished or made out to be more than it is?

I suspect that in a highly competitive society we're tempted to keep ramping up the rhetoric, warranted or not, to keep pace with our rivals. We fear that if we don't present something in the most hyperbolic terms no one will listen to us.

The opposite is true. We've hit the ceiling on superlatives. There's nowhere left to go. Our raves defy belief. Or elicit skepticism. Yet we keep slathering them on.

If everything we experience is "totally awesome," every product "industry leading," every new feature "game-changing," every other word "best, "simplest," "hottest," "coolest," "greatest," "whatever-est"...people tune out. It doesn't register. Sure, there's a possibility it could be true, but no one is going to accept it at face value. Not anymore.

The compulsion to overstate, perfume and bloviate ad nauseum in our communications is epidemic, either out of insecurity or an unwillingness to burn the extra brain cells to say something pithy and kickass. One way to break the habit is to stop using...

14 Lazy modifiers

Including the aforementioned superlatives, they're so-named because rather than express something in a refreshing way, the writer lazily tacks on a bankrupt adjective or adverb to do the work he or she didn't bother to. In the futile hope it might stick.

Examples:

BUSINESS BLATHER: "The service was quite slow." "The villagers were really poor." "The weather was very harsh."

Adverbs like "quite," "really," and "very" are lame tag-alongs. They suggest you lack faith the adjective they modify will do its job; or doubt your listener will get the extent of what you're saying. So you tack on a trite enhancer for insurance.

This actually can weaken your statement because it emasculates perfectly good descriptors that evolved primarily because they're powerful in themselves (rich, poor, difficult, easy, soft, hard, dirty, clean, kind, mean, fast, slow).

This may be a leap of faith, but reverting to simple, unvarnished assertions often packs more punch than using embellished ones:

BETTER: "The service was slow." "The villagers were poor." "The weather was harsh."

See the power in that? In most cases, the bare adjective wields more than enough clout to make your point.

Of course, there are situations when something stronger is preferred. In those cases, ditch the "really," the "very" and the "quite" and get creative. Try an analogy, a little wit or even sarcasm to drive home your message:

BETTER: "We had faster service at a snail convention."

Another example of a lazy modifier:

BUSINESS BLATHER: "Our sales increased a whopping 30%."

There's a tendency in business writing to spin a statement even before the audience has a chance to digest it. 30% is 30%. It could be great. Meh. Or ugly.

But it insults one's intelligence, and comes off more as opinion than fact, to jump in front of a number and presell it.

More credible, make the direct statement, then offer factual support for it:

BETTER: "Our sales increased 30%, exceeding all estimates."

The following statement is indicative of the dozens of wild, unsubstantiated claims we're exposed to daily, making nonbelievers of us all:

BUSINESS BLATHER: "We serve the tastiest donuts on the planet!"

Says who? By setting the bar at impossible heights, you're only setting your customers up for a letdown.

Yes, you may snare one-time purchasers, but even if the donuts are better than the guy's across town, people will likely be disappointed and resent your gulling them into buying one.

If you're going to rely on hyperbole, frame it in a way that's obvious in its overstatement, playful enough that customers will be amused by your farcical claim:

> BETTER: "Donuts so delicious, you'll never oversleep again."

See? And it didn't need a bang (!) at the end.

> TIP: Whatever you're reading, get into the habit of noting what words, sentences or passages strike paydirt with you, win a point, cause you to think "exactly!" Save those snippets to guide and inspire you to craft similar arguments and structures in your own writing. Conversely, note what has zero effect on you. Ask yourself why, then do your best to avoid such anemic expression.

Tired modifiers are ripe for the trash heap. Say things in imaginative ways. Surprise your audience. Coin new phrases. It's okay!

TIP: This book assumes you have basic writing, grammar and spelling skills—that you can string together words in a reasonably logical way, without typos, incorrect usage, poor sentence structure. If not, little I tell you here will matter. Take a course, read a book, bone up on your writing fundamentals. Use this as a companion guide to take your proficient written and verbal communications to a new level of clarity and creativity.

15 Avoid pack-mule sentences

Writing concisely doesn't mean stuffing everything into the same utterance. Especially if it contains sequences of abstract terms that force the reader to pause frequently to digest each and fathom how it relates to the whole:

BUSINESS BLATHER: Transform your management strategy through predictive intelligence that provides inventory visibility and data-rich insights delivered through a technology-enabled service to help streamline operations, lower costs, and deliver a better patient experience.

Gulp. Too much to swallow. Business communication is rife with obstacle-course sentences that, rather than flow smoothly with incremental meaning, are like picking your way barefoot along a path of sharp pebbles.

I have little idea what they were trying to convey in the above passage, but making some assumptions, it might be more clearly expressed like this:

BETTER: Predictive intelligence gathers data from past experience to accurately project future needs. This can help you control inventory, streamline operations, lower costs, and deliver a better patient experience.

Fewer words. More meaning. Nothing tops it.

TIP: Purists might note I split the infinitive "to accurately project." Once punishable by life imprisonment, infinitive splitting is now generally acceptable for two reasons: 1. It's a clearer way to express the thought. (Unsplit the infinitive by putting "accurately" after "needs," the emphasis winds up in the wrong place, if you see what I mean); and 2. It's taking conversational license—that is, rather than adhering to the King's English, you write in a way we normally speak to make it more relatable. But...

Tip: Conversational license doesn't condone bad grammar. It's one thing to connect with your audience using familiar language, like sentences without verbs, occasional slang for emphasis, creative punctuation, or other informalities. Just don't let it be an excuse to write sloppily. *Your readers will know the difference.*

16 Lose the jargon...or lose your audience

Undoubtedly you've been (or will be) in a business meeting where you haven't a clue what they're talking about. The conversation is riddled with acronyms, technical terms or insider vernacular. You sit there, fretting, praying you won't be called on for your input.

Communicating in industry jargon is okay when you're confident everyone will understand what you're articulating.

But a good chunk of the websites I visit or printed materials I read as a potential customer use obscure terminology or shop lingo they incorrectly assume prospects will comprehend.

Their loss. I have little patience for businesses turned so inwardly they fail to educate outsiders in a basic understanding of what their products are...and do.

Here's an example from a project management software website I was checking out to see if I could bring a little sanity to the smorgasbord of assignments I undertake. Things pretty much made sense until I came upon this:

BUSINESS BLATHER: [Headline] Create Task Dependencies to Save Time. [Text] Utilize powerful features such as Task Dependencies, so that you can move dates for hundreds of tasks in one click.

That was it. No further explanation. Now, maybe I'm a hayseed (though I grew up in the city), but never have I stumbled upon the term "task dependency." Is it a condition workaholics suffer from? Is it a person who's the only one can get a particular thing done?

Wrong on both counts. To understand what I was being sold, I had to leave the page entirely to google "task dependency." Thus apprised, this is how I would have described the feature:

> **BETTER: Create Task Dependencies—tasks that need to start or finish before others can proceed—a powerful tool for setting priorities, automatically adjusting dates, saving time, and managing projects more efficiently.**

You never want to leave a perfectly viable prospect in the dark about what you're offering. Because most people aren't going to take the time to look it up as I did. In those instances, an important selling point is squandered.

Multiply this little incident by the billions of other miscommunications and non-communications occurring daily, you get a sense of how much business is lost to overestimating your audience's knowledge level.

Sometimes your customers may be tech-heads—like engineers, medical professionals, IT technicians—who love drilling down into the details and specs before they buy.

Fine. Have at it. But don't forget. The nontechnical CEO who came from sales, or the finance guy who controls the purse strings, might be the ones making the final purchasing decision.

So while you don't want to dumb down your presentation to a fourth-grade level, at least make it understandable enough so *any* interested party knows what they're coughing up the dough for.

17 Avoid salvage jobs. *Start fresh*

I belong to one of those professions where many of my clients fancy they can do it themselves. They wouldn't dare perform a dental procedure on their tooth. They'd freak if the pilot on their flight asked them to help out in the cockpit.

But when it comes to writing copy they're self-proclaimed wordsmiths. They'll send me a terrible draft prefaced with "it just needs a little editing."

I suspect this is as much to knock down my price as anything else. But I never buy it. I tell them I only write original copy, from the ground up, to establish a unique style and cohesiveness throughout. Which is true.

Then I hit them with the fee-protecting clincher: to edit it to my liking would probably take longer (cost more) than starting from scratch, and I wouldn't be as happy with it. Also true. Like rebuilding a car part by part. It will never be like new.

That usually secures the assignment. *And the fee.*

Lesson: unless you're a professional editor with zero time for rewrites, start fresh. Consider what's given you as merely input, even if they say "it's almost there." It's never almost there.

Good writing takes talent, certainly, but also an acquired ability to weave disparate elements cohesively into a "hey, this is really good!" piece.

Take it from the top. You'll be far more pleased with the outcome than a glorified cut-and-paste job, and enjoy the process immeasurably more.

18 "Purposeful" and other words without purpose

While there are instances where the word "purposeful" works (she led a purposeful life), the way it's used in business is often meaningless:

BUSINESS BLATHER: We had a purposeful meeting.

As opposed to what? Having one just for kicks? To shoot the breeze? Kill time?

BETTER: We had a productive meeting.

Another head-scratcher is "core competency." A LinkedIn profile might read:

BUSINESS BLATHER: Communication is one of my core competencies.

Great, you can talk! Why don't you also mention that you're toilet trained, able to find your way to the office, can tie your shoes, and other core competencies?

Being merely competent in something (Dictionary.com defines it as "adequate but not exceptional") is a low bar to set for yourself. Adding "core," meaning basic, lowers it even further.

Somewhere, someone once coined the term "core competency." It sounded good so everyone jumped on it, not realizing it's not a flattering claim. Time to let it go:

BETTER: I excel at communication.

"Results driven" is another empty phrase rampant in the job search market. People see other candidates using it so why not them, too?

It begs the sarcastic response: "Oh, you're results driven? Sorry, we're actually looking for slackers who aren't interested in accomplishing anything. But thanks for applying."

Instead of saying you're results driven, why not include some results you were driven to achieve? (More about showing results in the LinkedIn Profile section in Part Two.)

I realize these expressions fit comfortably like a worn shoe, but that's the problem. You want to break out of that comfort zone, avoid staleness, predictability and...

19 Everybodyism

"Well, everyone else is saying it" has to be the lamest reason for saying something. You want to say things *no one* else is. That's how you capture attention, implant your message into another's consciousness.

Everybodyism might feel safe, noncontentious, conforming. But as a writing or speaking strategy? Deadly.

It leans on the crutch of familiarity, which as we know breeds contempt. It risks your assertions fading into the drab background of sameness.

I wince when I hear expressions like "going forward" because it's overused, redundant if you're already using future tense, and blunts the impact of the statement you're making:

BUSINESS BLATHER: This will be a great addition to our office going forward.

BETTER: This will be a great addition to our office.

Or It gets in the way of making a punchier declaration:

BUSINESS BLATHER: Going forward, we'll be taking a more aggressive sales approach.

BETTER: Buckle up. We'll be taking a more aggressive sales approach.

And lest we forget that shopworn closing to almost every discussion—instead of:

BUSINESS BLATHER: At the end of the day, our platform delivers more savings than competing software programs.

Say something more germane to the topic:

BETTER: When you add up the benefits, our platform delivers more savings than competing software programs.

Carefully review what you've written to see if any of these kinds of clichés have snuck in there. Replace them with something fresher, something everybody else *isn't* saying.

20 The endless anguish over "value proposition" and like phrases

"Value proposition" is a term that has companies turning

themselves inside out, spending wads of money in the process, trying to answer the existential question: "What is our value proposition?" Like a mystic pondering, "What is it all about?"

I avoid the expression—and others like it—because its abstract nature invites the creation of reams of cerebral business blather in the form of focus groups, reports, presentations, theories, discussions, analyses, and strategizing ad nauseum.

Granted, the eternal quest to know one's value proposition creates jobs, indeed industries, but seriously, is it really that complicated?

Save your money. Come right out with it:

Your value proposition, in all its stripped down nakedness, is the benefit you offer your customers.

If you don't know what that is, why did you start the business in the first place?

Just ask the kooky creative ensconced in a tiny cubicle at your ad agency what your value proposition is. He or she will nail it in a day or two, manifest in a killer ad campaign.

Yes, I'm oversimplifying it, but I would wager that the guy who created the iconic "Where's the beef?" campaign for Wendy's didn't hatch it by poring over mountains of data analyses and doctoral-length theses.

Lesson: Avoid nebulous theoretical terms that trigger a chain reaction of equally nebulous dissertations trying to explain them.

21 Acronym acrimony

I find myself constantly googling acronyms (initialed abbreviations) for their meaning. You, too? Exasperating isn't it?

Business jargon is so fraught with them, it's almost impossible to keep up with their onslaught. Especially those you come upon infrequently enough you completely forget what they stand for next time they pop up.

Then there are acronyms that can mean more than one thing. Just ask organizations that used to go by the initials WTF about that.

Before you infuse your document or oral presentation with acronyms, be sure your audience will understand them. You don't want to pepper an uninitiated prospect with something like this:

> **BUSINESS BLATHER: Our SaaS package includes a CMS that can greatly improve your KPIs.**

What rolls easily off your tongue or keyboard might be a brain teaser for others. It never hurts to be on the safe side and use the long form:

BETTER: Our software-as-a-service package includes a content management system that can greatly improve your key performance indicators.

If you're making repeated use of the term, include the full meaning the first time, then revert to just the acronym:

BETTER: Our software-as-a-service (SaaS) package includes a content management system (CMS) that can greatly improve your key performance indicators (KPIs).

Hmm, even that sounds overly acronymic. Try to use them sparingly, if possible?

22 Format your text for readability

Today, we need to be more than writers. Fussy readers dictate we become typographical designers. Long, plain-vanilla blocks of uninterrupted text just aren't sexy. A drudge to read.

Copy needs to appeal to the eye, invite you in, offer enough variation to keep you engaged.

This can be done with shorter paragraphs of differing sizes, occasional indents, emboldened type, clipped sentences.

(That's how this book is designed. Hope the format is working for you.)

If everything you're currently writing looks as indomitable as the El Capitan massif at Yosemite, you need to break it up a bit.

Examine text treatments online and off. Note what kind of formatting appeals to you, makes you want to dive in and read.

Then incorporate those styles into your own work.

23 Content vs. copy: know the difference

Do you want your communications to inform? Or sell?

There's a difference between content writing (informational) and copywriting (promotional). Different purpose. Different talents required. Different writing skills involved.

Content writing educates. It takes an objective, journalistic approach, providing expert information and advice on the topic covered.

Blogs, white papers, e-zines, articles, informational videos, podcasts, and newsletters are good examples.

The strength of content writing lies in its ability to gain the trust of your target through unbiased analysis of a product or category. No opinions, please.

Copywriting, on the other hand, is *intended* to sell. It engages the prospect with a provocative concept, describes features and benefits of the product or service in powerful ways, and closes the pitch by strongly urging the customer to take action.

Commercial websites, print ads, social media ads, online display ads, email campaigns, direct mail, and brochures are just a few examples.

Unquestionably, you should use both forms of writing in your marketing campaigns. It's just as important to establish yourself as a subject matter expert in your industry through content writing as it is to sell your wares through copywriting.

While copywriting often contains impartial content in support of its unabashed sales pitch, not so the other way around.

Be careful not to inject your purportedly unbiased content with blatant promotional material lest you erode the confidence of your reader or listener.

Many good content writers believe they can readily transition into copywriting. Easier said than done.

Effective ad copy takes a different mindset and skillset developed over time. It's more creative, engaging, emotional. That comes with practice and experience.

Read ads. Pay attention to TV commercials. Open that envelope promoting pet health insurance even though all you have is a goldfish.

See what sells *you*. Great advertising looks simple, but is less so to create.

I show you how to hone both your content writing and copywriting skills for different types of media in Part Two.

24 Forget deadlines, try "startlines"

For a society so obsessed with when a project gets finished, we're curiously all too casual about when to get it started.

Procrastinating until it's almost too late is a major reason many written communications, presentations and speeches are so incoherently constructed and flat-out dull.

If you constantly put yourself under the gun and leave little time to create, you're going to revert to the corporate blather you're comfortable with just to get it done. Not good.

Instead of stressing over when something is due, focus on getting it underway.

Set a "startline." That is, the time by which it's essential you get a project started, so it isn't executed in a rushed and slapdash manner.

If you stick to your startline, it not only assures efficient, unhurried performance, it all but eliminates the need for a deadline...and the anxiety that goes with it.

Which "line" would you rather work under? *Get it started.*

PART TWO BETTER COMMUNICATION. IN ALL ITS FORMS.

LINKEDIN PROFILES

25 Let's get your own house in order first

If you want to write better business communications, a great place to start—no, the *best* place to start—is your LinkedIn profile.

The LinkedIn profile is arguably the most misunderstood, underutilized, undervalued tool in the business arsenal.

With over three quarters of a *billion* LinkedIn members, you think people would take the platform more seriously.

But for some reason, the coconut has yet to fall from the tree and knock some sense into those failing to harness the awesome power of this dominant business portal. Especially when it's free.

Whether you know it or not, like it or not, ever increasing numbers of recruiters, coworkers, colleagues, clients, bosses, friends, strangers, prospective landlords, mortgage lenders, and old high school flames are checking you out on LinkedIn.

So you don't want to greet them with a profile the equivalent of answering the door in your pajamas. Or worse, no profile at all.

A huge chunk of those 750 million LinkedIn profiles are so uninspired, I started a healthy ancillary business writing them.

Scores of profiles later, I have these tips and caveats to share:

26 You're not using *that* for a profile pic, are you?

This doesn't have to do with the writing, but visitors to your LinkedIn page may not get that far if your profile image is a dud.

Would you show up for a job interview with a glass of wine in your hand? Then don't be holding one in your profile pic!

Or use a crudely cropped snapshot with someone's fingers curled around your shoulder. A plant growing out of your head. A fluorescent light reflecting off your forehead. Or a creepy looking guy lurking in the shadows behind you.

Get the picture? Then get serious. Hire a photographer.

LinkedIn research shows: profiles with professional headshots receive 14 times more views and are 36 times more likely to elicit a response.

Even more if you're smiling. (Aloof, I'm-a-badass poses and tight-lipped expressions don't cut it on LinkedIn. Looking friendly and approachable does.)

27 That bland default background image? *Lose it*

It makes you blend in with the millions of others who don't bother to change theirs, or don't realize they can.

Again, here's where studies show you can boost your profile readership significantly. Choose a dramatic shot of your geographic area, something related to your profession, your business's logo or products, a striking abstract pattern, or maybe a quote that fits you to a T.

Make sure the background image goes nicely with your profile pic.

Now that your masthead is a visual stunner, let's keep the momentum going with some dazzling prose.

28 Your headline says it all. Or *not*

If you want your LinkedIn profile to win over a recruiter, potential client or colleague, it has to start with your headline.

It's the first thing visitors read, the first impression you make on the world. So take every creative advantage of the 240 characters you're allotted to make it sing.

Most users just slug in their title and company:

BUSINESS BLATHER: Controller, XYZ Inc.

Borrring. That leaves about 220 characters of brilliant, keyword-rich self-promotion untapped. Don't squander it:

BETTER: **Controller of Multimillion Dollar Company with Expertise in Taxes and Financial Analysis Excels at Cutting Costs, Streamlining Processes and Reducing Waste.**

Even if you're not presently looking for a job (or are, but don't want anyone to know), it pays to have a strong headline that makes you "discoverable."

You never know when a recruiter might approach you with a dream job. Or upper management is considering you for a promotion. Best to always look your best.

Now, suppose you actually are in the market for a new position and not presently working for anyone. Don't make people guess. Come right out and let them know you're available:

BETTER: **Elite Sales Executive with Excellent Record of Success Growing Revenues and Expanding Territories Seeks New Opportunity.**

Work hard on your headline. It's the door that either entices visitors to enter and find out more about you...or turns them away.

29 About the all-important "About" section

This is your chance to shine, tell your story, reel off your greatest hits, be a name dropper, showcase your unique talents and skills.

The About (or summary) section gives you 2,600 characters, roughly 350-400 words, to engage, inform and sell your audience. Use as many as needed to wow them without being a chatterbox.

Top-load the section with any well-known companies you worked for; your most salient achievements; honors, awards and special recognition you received; notable schools you studied at; degrees you earned. Put them in order of prominence, not chronologically.

I call it the Harvard effect. If someone reveals to you right off they went to Harvard, you can bet everything they say after that will carry more weight.

While maybe not as impressive, we all have a Harvard-like boast or two that will add a positive sheen to the rest of our profile. So put it right up front.

And yes, I said boast. Your profile is one place where humility can take a backseat. If you did something outstanding, rightly take credit for it.

Recruiters and employers aren't looking for timid, self-effacing people. As I say to my clients, if you don't toot your own horn, the person who ultimately gets the job probably did.

Yet inexplicably, the vast majority of LinkedIn users leave their About section blank, incomplete or hopelessly dull.

Many merely snip passages from their resumes, filled with nonspecifics like:

> **BUSINESS BLATHER: Skilled, forward-thinking IT professional with proven track record is a collaborative team player and problem solver. Especially skilled at analyzing problems, developing and simplifying procedures, and creating innovative solutions. Reliable, professional and friendly.**

That's all he wrote—269 characters out of thousands available.

Now, to be fair, this wouldn't be that bad if tens of millions of other LinkedIn users weren't, believe me, saying the same thing. Making the same unsupported claims.

If anyone with a vested interest in viewing your profile knows one thing, as I said in Part One: you are not something simply because you say you are.

Show me the money. Where's the evidence? What problems did you solve? What procedures did you simplify? What innovative solutions did you create? Be specific.

As importantly, who are you? How did you get to where you are? What is your approach to your work, your career, your life? Again, specifics please.

Here's the profile of a woman in sales with a compelling story to tell, that ultimately landed her a position she loves:

BETTER:

When you're selling product to Schlumberger, Northrop Grumman, Pride International, Ensco Drilling, and other industry leaders, you better know what you're doing.

More than that, you better excel at building relationships, provide unswerving customer service, work your tail off, be willing to travel, and, equally important, be likable!

Fortunately, I've been able to cultivate all of those qualities. And it didn't happen by luck. Or overnight.

I got my baptism by fire right out of school, joining Advance Steel Supply, where I virtually single-handedly oversaw customer service, sales, purchasing, inventory control, receivables, payables, payroll, staff training...an extraordinary educational foundation on which I built a successful career in sales.

"Anne's greatest asset...is Anne herself," wrote my CEO. "Her personality is a boost to any business. Customers love dealing with her."

My extra-mile work ethic is ingrained. Family need demanded I work 32 hours a week while attending high school. I persevered. And still found time to work with athletes in the Special Olympics. They inspired me. If they didn't shrink from a challenge, no matter how daunting, how could I?

While forging my career, I grabbed every opportunity to expand my business acumen, including night school, professional development programs, technical courses. If it helped boost my contributions to my employer, and advance my career, I was in.

The last few years I've plied my talents successfully to my own business, in the investment, refurbishment and sale of real estate.

Now, ready to reenter the corporate world, I seek a position that can fully benefit from my skills, experience and drive. And yes, I will travel.

People love to be told a story. We are so much more than a bunch of bullet points. The above summary puts a human face on Anne, helps you learn some interesting things about her, makes her more accessible, believable, *hirable*.

You also have a story to tell. Let the world hear it!

30 Optimizing your Experience section

Here's where you get to present your work history in chronological order, including your title, company, dates, location, and a description of what you did at each position.

But don't for a minute think you can just cut and paste chunks of your resume and be done with it. Unless you want to risk being overlooked.

I say this because today's resumes (and I read many) seem to be getting longer and longer, duller and duller, becoming lengthy day-in-the-life-of descriptions of duties that must leave recruiters who receive hundreds of them daily catatonic.

The resume is basically a compilation and formatting task. The profile a creative writing one.

Lengthy bulleted lists of every last function you were assigned, whether in your resume or profile, beg to go unread.

Further, they focus more on the quantity of your work rather than how well you performed.

I'll spare you an example of this, but you can well imagine how people might get carried away trying to impress others with the sheer volume of tasks they juggled. I caution my clients not to fall into that trap.

Instead, to help them get their Experience section actually read, I developed a format that, for each position, highlights the *major* responsibilities their employer entrusted them with, and the *results* of what their efforts achieved.

It goes something like this:

BETTER:

RESPONSIBILITIES: At this leading recruitment agency, I was charged with managing the business development and service functions to spur the long-term growth of the company. This demanded of me a mastery of interpersonal, creative and leadership skills to develop sales strategies, reach out to industry leaders, deliver compelling presentations, and ensure our team followed through on meeting our clients' objectives.

RESULTS: Overall, I secured over $250 million in agency revenues. I oversaw the creation of the firm's lead protocols and database. I generated qualified leads across all industries, especially companies within the Fortune 1000. And my process improvements were a boon to the profitability of my agency.

The format is one that allows readers to quickly zero in on key information to get a quick take on you. If they want further details, they can always drill down on the resume itself, which, by the way, can be uploaded to your profile:

> **TIP: Right below the About section in the Featured section, and for each position in the Experience section, LinkedIn allows you to upload images, videos and documents, as well as insert links to websites and other media. It's an excellent way to furnish visual proof of your accomplishments, such as awards, letters of appreciation, article clippings, product literature, anything that adds interest and enhances your credibility and credentials.**

31 Don't shortchange the Education, Volunteer and other sections

In addition to the schools you studied at, include any relevant clubs, teams and extracurricular activities you participated in, and positions of leadership you might have held, especially if you're just starting out in your career.

In the Volunteer section, even if it was only a one-day stint at Habitat for Humanity many years ago, put it in. You don't have to give dates or length of the service.

And of course, include any school, church, community, sports, or company-sponsored volunteer work you performed. If you did it, get credit for it. It does make an impression.

There are other sections, too, for listing licenses and certifications, honors and awards, articles you've written, professional development courses you've taken, organizations you belong to, skills you possess, and more. You never know which credential will push you over the top in another's esteem and prompt them to click on your contact info.

Spend the time to make your profile as complete as possible. You'll be rewarded with higher rankings in LinkedIn searches, more views and maybe even a lucrative job offer coming out of nowhere.

WEBSITES

32 Does your website woo visitors...or shoo them?

Your homepage is the store window the world peers through to get a glimpse of what you're offering. So it's essential you display quick, clear enticements to pull people in.

Yet, you'd think some websites were created with the express purpose of making visitors go away. Their headlines are clichés, generic, unclear, or too coy for their own good.

Take for instance a site that greets you with words like these:

BUSINESS BLATHER: We offer business solutions that increase productivity, simplify your workload and improve your bottom line.

That's the headline. What's so bad about that, you wonder. Well, consider:

If you sold pencils on a street corner, this statement could apply. If you dealt in industrial supercomputers, ditto. Likewise with virtually any other B2B enterprise in captivity.

So why should I be lured in by the same bland, worn-out claim gazillions of companies are making when they haven't even told me what the heck they're selling?

Your headline is the most precious piece of real estate on your website. Nothing comes close to its importance because it's your make-or-break opportunity to hook your visitor and get them to explore further. Blow it, they'll be history in a heartbeat.

For heaven's sake, let people know, in no uncertain terms, where they are, what you're dealing in, and what's in it for them:

BETTER: Our groundbreaking software for real estate developers fully automates every aspect of the projects you undertake.

Now, if I were a homebuilder, that headline might strike a nerve the hackneyed "business solutions" blather would not.

Another nonstarter, and I would guess this is the most widely used headline on the web, is "Welcome."

Cordial of you, but a sterling opportunity to impart vital information about your product or service...*squandered.*

If you were investing $60,000 in a full-page magazine ad, would your headline be "Welcome"? Pretend you're shelling out that kind of money when creating your homepage header.

In all likelihood it'll be a good one.

33 Be on the same page as your visitor.

Should your website be a single page or multiple pages?

SEO (search engine optimization) specialists say you'll rank higher in searches if your site is spread over several pages.

But many website owners and writers want to control the presentation, not have the visitor clicking haphazardly and disrupting the flow of the pitch. So they opt for the all-inclusive scroll-down one-pager.

Why not have both? And not in a redundant way.

For example, the homepage would give the reader in digest format all the key info—product, features, benefits, call to action—they would need to make a decision and click the "Buy Now" button, complete the response form, or call the toll-free number.

In other words, a self-contained sales page akin to the drive-thru window at a fast food restaurant.

If people want to explore further, supporting pages would furnish more in-depth material—say, comprehensive product details, company philosophy, bios of key personnel, news, blog entries— things that can trigger higher rankings in searches.

> **TIP: If possible, put your response mechanism on every page—top, bottom or wherever it works best. You want to be right there the very moment your prospect entertains an urge to act. This also makes your call to action available if the visitor happens to arrive at your site on a subpage (and some will). I'm dumbfounded how many websites leave you floundering when you're ready to pounce but can't find the friggin' checkout. (Of course, then you're called to dinner, your enthusiasm wanes and they've blown an easy sale.)**

34 Your website should be blemish-free

Would you show up for a sales meeting with a lipstick smudge on your front tooth? A stain on your shirt? Then why display a website riddled with typos, grammatical errors, uneven spacing, weirdly formatted text, and other irritating distractions?

Unfortunately, the bar has been set low for these kinds of things. Which makes for a distasteful visitor experience. Yet many web creators either don't care or think this is an acceptable level of presentation.

And that's a good thing for you. Why? Because when you clean up the typographical mess that may be your website, you'll stand out like a newly minted coin in a pile of tarnished pennies.

Strive to make your web copy as readably perfect as it is engagingly written. You'd be surprised how many people notice these things and how it reflects positively on your credibility and reputation.

It takes a keen eye and a minimal amount of time to get it right.

EMAILS

35 Your inbox is an education

To get a good idea of how *not* to write a business email, all you need to do is turn a critical eye on the piles of them you're pelted with daily (for office workers that's an average of 121), whether client communications, interoffice correspondence, pings from colleagues, promotions from companies you do business with, or never-ending spam.

Note how ridiculously long some of them are, that presume you have this luxury of time to indulge their verbosity. How poorly others are written. How some try to gull you with bogus flattery. Or leave you cold. Or make no sense at all.

Merely canvassing your inbox can be an instructive experience. Be mindful of the impression each message makes on you, what turns you on, or off, which ones you're enticed to open, which you can't delete fast enough, and which state their purpose clearly and persuasively.

That's a good start. Here are other guidelines to help you become an ace email communicator.

36 Subject lines

Subject lines are the "Hey, guess what?" of email communications.

Studies that analyzed billions of emails came up with general findings about what kind of subject lines trigger the most opens.

Among them: length of about 3 to 5 words (up to 55 characters), Using Initial Caps Like This, including the recipient's name if possible, citing numbers, plus loads of other suggestions. Just google something like "subject lines that work best."

Keep in mind, these are general guidelines. A clever, well-crafted subject line customized to the purpose at hand will usually beat out a formulaic one.

In conducting day-to-day business—that is, communicating with coworkers, supervisors, clients, vendors, industry colleagues, and the like—subject lines need only clearly indicate what you're writing about. That and your recognizable email address should ensure the message will be opened.

More ingenuity is needed when pitching a product or service cold to potential business clients or consumers. The trick here is to craft a subject line with a strong enticement without being spammy.

Yes, it's okay to use a teaser, but never with a false or deceptive claim that isn't paid off inside. Recipients will feel used. You will immediately lose trust. Be clever, but be honest is a good strategy to go by.

As covered in the previous section, you can learn a lot from the subject lines of the emails you receive.

Which ones encourage you to open them? Do they follow through on the promise they make? Which ooze snake oil, are weakly expressed, make ridiculous claims, insult your intelligence, are raunchy or disrespectful?

Here are a few subject lines plucked from my inbox that rightly deserved relegation to the trash bin:

BUSINESS BLATHER:

Congratulations! We've been trying to reach you. Please respond! [No thanks]

Deleting this email could cost you thousands of dollars. [My loss]

Make your partner scream with pleasure nightly. [In my dreams]

And here are some that piqued my curiosity enough to take a peek inside:

BETTER:

Time for some traffic problems on your website...

SEO In A Nutshell (actually, a little ebook)

Is Your Garage Usable...Or Inexcusable?

Live-Streaming Workouts Are In. Are You?

37 The email body: state your business, please

The inside of the email is where many go off the rails. Just because someone opened a message doesn't mean they'll put up with blabbermouth self-indulgence.

Fail to fulfill the subject line promise immediately, your recipient will dump you in a flash to address the many other messages cluttering their inbox.

Here's a basic formula I use—whether a simple text email or graphic html—that's worked well both for my own business and for my clients. I'll give you an example in a sec, but this is basically what the email body entails:

1. Convey your message in as few words as possible, ideally 150 or fewer.

2. Put your most potent selling point up front.

3. Right after that, to entice an early click, insert a link to your landing page. (Rather than a text link I prefer the actual URL, which can be copied and pasted if necessary.)

4. Add more selling points or expand on the main one. *Briefly.*

5. Reprise the landing page link.

6. Say goodbye and (optional) add a postscript with a phone number.

Here's the email body of a message from a financial advisor prospecting for clients:

[First Name],

Living long is good. Outliving your money? Not so good. To learn how you might, and how to avoid it, download your FREE report:

https://companyname.com/report

In "Outliving Your Money" the harsh realities of retirement saving are exposed.

But take comfort. You CAN overcome them. *If you start now.* In this breakout report we reveal:

-- The biggest threats to a secure retirement
-- The challenge of calculating how long you'll live
-- 3 things you can do to make your money last
-- Minimize market risk to ensure lifelong income
-- And more

Look, you can blow this off with a vague promise to address it later.

Or get serious. Invest the 15 minutes it takes to read this life-changing report:

https://companyname.com/report

Here's to a long and happy retirement.

[Advisor Name and Company]

P.S. Please call me with questions: [000-000-0000]

PRESS RELEASES

38 What it takes to create the buzz

A press release can be a powerhouse tool for promoting your brand, products, news, special deals, events, and more.

But it will flop. *Unless...*

Unless it ignites curiosity. Makes a deeper human connection than the thousands of lifeless releases shotgun-blasted into the cosmos each day, begging to be ignored.

Unless it's engaging to read. No cram-everything-in headline that makes little sense. No painfully dull prose that doubles as a sleeping aid. No self-promoting fluff respectable media outlets toss posthaste into the trash.

Unless it makes a crazy-busy editor's job ridiculously easy. Meaning, offering them a tight, well-crafted story they don't have to take a hatchet to, one they can slug right in and run with.

39 It starts with your header

An immediate tipoff a press release isn't worth reading is the headline.

Many are so loaded with names, places, details, and keywords in an attempt to cover every base in one gasp...they're virtually incomprehensible. Unless you enjoy cracking codes. Here's an example of one that just can't contain itself:

> **BUSINESS BLATHER: Ideanomics (NASDAQ: IDEX) Reports Qingdao City Construction Investment Group Enters into Cooperation Agreement with Sun Seven Stars Investment Group to Fund and Finance Ideanomics' EV Sales**

Yikes, and that's just the headline. If you're writing solely to flag down search engine spiders that never get bored, go for it. But don't expect real people to dive in.

Upon skimming the release for insight, what might have been more inviting to the audience it targets is a headline like this:

> **BETTER: Ideanomics Secures $7 Billion to Fund Electric Vehicle Purchases**

Your headline should only be as long as it continues to hold interest and make sense. Translation: as short as possible. Work on it. Nothing will have more impact on the success of the release.

40 The press release body: stick to the facts

Imagine a news anchor reporting an armed robbery at a local restaurant, then in all seriousness adding: "And by the way, you should try the cheese blintzes. Delicious."

That's what many press releases have become: shameless editorializing, blatant advertisements, far removed from the relatively objective news stories they once were.

Owe it to competing wire services vying for clients, and trade publications hungry for advertisers, that are delighted to run just about anything short of a manifesto to overthrow the government.

If you want your release to be an outright sales pitch, there are plenty of outlets happy to oblige. They'll even write it for you.

But if you have a truly compelling story to tell, the best chance of it being picked up by a major news organization is to craft it like a respected journalist would.

Which is not to say it can't be creatively told, or even have biased commentary in it. You do that by salting the release with quotes from key individuals related to the story. So the opinions are coming from them, not the one who's reporting them.

A vast amount of business releases are self-congratulatory pats on the back—employees promoted, awards won, recognition received, targets hit, milestones reached.

Whatever the purpose, each is an opportunity to go beyond the humdrum and convey your newsworthy item in a relatable and maybe even novel way.

Remember, as with other forms of writing discussed in this book, always be guided by the questions: What would *you* want to read? What would hold *your* interest?

Here are two examples of press releases radically different in style, yet each effectively fulfilling its mission.

The first takes a classic approach, containing all the required elements in conveying the who, what, when, where, and why in a straightforward, informative manner (note, names and location have been changed for confidentiality):

Wellness Clinic Reverses Loss of Sex Drive with New Hormone Therapies

Summary: Using natural bioidentical hormones derived from plants, the New Life Anti-Aging Clinic restores healthy testosterone and estrogen levels in men and women to improve sexual vitality.

Locustville, Wisconsin (June 10, 20XX) – To treat diminished sex drive, loss of energy and other debilitating symptoms of hormone imbalances, New Life Anti-Aging

Clinic now offers Bioidentical Hormone Replacement Therapy, or BHRT, to its male and female patients.

Bioidentical hormones, derived from plants, are identical in chemical structure and function to those produced by humans naturally—unlike animal-based and lab-synthesized hormones that may act differently in the body.

In the BHRT procedure, rice-sized pellets are implanted under the skin where they release a steady flow of hormones over a 3 to 4 month period. These include bioidentical estrogen (Estriol and Estradiol) that relieves hot flashes, nights sweats and other symptoms of menopause, as well as provides cardiovascular benefits and protection against osteoporosis.

Bioidentical testosterone pellets increase energy, muscle mass, bone density and sex drive in men, and in smaller amounts offer similar benefits and mood enhancement in women. Hormone pellets are custom formulated for each patient based on lab results, weight, height, and gender.

"BHRT pellet implantation is a painless, precise and effective procedure for restoring energy and an active sex life lost through hormonal imbalance," says M. Robert Gupta, Doctor of Osteopathic Medicine at the New Life clinic. "Treatments are needed only 3 to 4 times a year, compared to frequently having to apply messy creams or undergoing weekly injections."

For those whose estrogen is too high, Dr. Gupta can prescribe an anti-estrogen pellet to lower the level of the hormone. A simple blood test can determine a patient's current hormone levels, and a plan for treatment developed based on the findings.

According to the clinic, whether caused by a medical condition or the natural process of aging, hormone imbalances and their symptoms can be successfully reversed through long-lasting BHRT pellet implants.

For a free consultation, appointment or media inquiry visit (web address) or call 000-000-0000.

The second press release states its case more imaginatively, promoting an entity called halfbirthday.com. The release has fun with a fun topic, written in a style targeting parenting publications and blogs to garner the free press and publicity it received:

Oh Baby! Six Months Old. Where's the Party?

New York, New York (November 5, 20XX) – Six months. 180+ days. Twenty-six weeks. Half a year. Call it what you will, to a baby that's like...*forever*.

A hard-won accomplishment. A major milestone in their little life. Begs a celebration, wouldn't you think? A half birthday party, to be specific.

And not just for baby. Parents deserve a little pat on the rear, too. Think of the hundreds of diapers negotiated. Feedings dispensed. Burps elicited. Countless hours of sleep forfeited.

Is it any wonder hordes of moms and dads aren't waiting till the big oh-one and are raising sippy cups to toast the half-year mark?

Just googling or Twitter-searching "half birthday" will clue you in on how enthusiastically people are embracing this burgeoning occasion, and the thousands of interesting ways they're celebrating it.

At halfbirthday.com, headquarters for everything half birthday, visitors will encounter selections of half b'day gifts for all ages, half birthday party ideas and supplies, a half birthday calculator, recipes, games, and more.

Nice part is, a half-birthday fling doesn't have to be an all-out bash like a first birthday party. We're talking half here. Keep it relaxed, informal, inexpensive.

Instead of mailed invitations, evites will do fine. Only fun gifts with a "half" theme costing $10 tops allowed.

Refreshments? You need only go half out for this. Half a

ration of juice for the honoree and her little guests, half caffe coffee for the adults, half a cake, and an hour and a half at the most will result in a whole lot of fun.

As for decorations and activities, again let half, and your imagination, be your guide. You'll be surprised what neat ideas you hatch when you get going on this.

To see what other parents are doing to celebrate baby's midway day, and share in the ineffable joys they're experiencing at this stage in their child's development, visit halfbirthday.com.

For media inquiries, contact (email address).

PRESENTATIONS

41 Creating presentable presentations

I'm not going to spend a lot time on presentations. *You are.*

As I emphasized in Part One: clear, powerful, *concise* writing takes more time than lengthier drafts. Nothing is more true than when putting together an in-person, online or print presentation.

Once upon a time, before the advent of ubiquitous distractions and nonstop interruptions, an audience might be forgiving of a windbag session.

No more. To keep participants from tuning out, sneaking out or fiddling with their phones, you have to work extra hard to hold their attention.

That means no long leadups to your core points. No irrelevant filler that adds little support to your arguments. No text-heavy slides whose content vanishes from memory the moment the next one loads.

Here are the kind of phrases to avoid when giving your presentation that are sure tipoffs you're veering off course and risking muffled groans from your audience:

BUSINESS BLATHER:

"Bear with me a few minutes while we explore..."

"First, let's go back and see how this all came about..."

"There are fifteen things you need to be aware of..."

"Let's take a detailed look at the numbers..."

"Our company's mission is based on five distinct philosophies..."

Ugh. Spare your victims the anguish. Skip the BS. Lose the tedious background baloney:

BETTER: "I know your time is valuable, so I'll get right to the point."

Then say something momentous. Disruptive. Even controversial.

Keep it upbeat, dramatic, succinct. Surprise, excite, Illuminate. And sum up.

Then open it to questions. If they want more, they'll ask!

42 Make it interactive

If you haven't noticed, this is an interactive world. There are more ways than ever to interface with others.

To expect your audience to sit there like manikins while you jabber on is inviting disconnect. People want to be involved. In fact, some probably think they could give your presentation better than you can.

So let them. The more you engage people, the more they'll respond, stay awake, soak up your message.

It's an old trick that never fails to work because everyone likes to show off their knowledge. Instead of opening with:

BUSINESS BLATHER: "Today, I'm going to discuss the various ways to advertise and how you can blah, blah blah..."

Reel them in with something like:

> **BETTER: "Question. What do you think are the most cost-effective ways to advertise in today's marketplace? Who can name one of them for me?"**

Now, wait until you've receive several possible answers before revealing what the best ones are, allowing a number of people to participate.

Do this throughout your presentation. Also, ask questions that require a show of hands. Ask attendees to relate personal experiences that prove your points.

Time will fly. Your audience will do a lot of the work for you, have more fun, stay attentive, and your gig will be a success.

Please! Keep your presentations lean, energetic, involving.

ADVERTISING

43 Online display and social media ads

Writers of internet banner ads, or Facebook, Instagram and LinkedIn ads, face a thorny issue:

People hate online ads.

The click-through rate for display ads—those omnipresent website banners that come in all shapes and sizes—is about .05%, or one click for every 2,000 "ad impressions" (a euphemistic term that should more aptly be called "ad exposures," since overwhelmingly they *don't* make an impression).

If you wonder why the rate is so low, notice how, when you're intent on reading the content of a webpage, you don't even realize the ads are there.

That's why advertisers often use images of gnarly-faced old geezers, cute dogs, suggestively clad (or unclad) people, or animations that have nothing to do with the ad but supposedly draw your attention. The tactic is known as borrowed interest, it's been around forever, and people resent it.

Social media ads, placed smack in your newsfeed so you're sure to trip over them, score better with a 1.3% click-through.

You might think it doesn't matter what type of gimmick you use to provoke a glance and induce a click. That precious click.

It does. For a couple of reasons.

One, you don't want to be paying what could amount to a hefty charge for those clicking solely out of artificially induced curiosity, who have little idea what you're selling, much less an interest in buying. That gets expensive, be assured.

Two, this is why people hate online advertising. The deceptions, the come-ons, the clickbait erode credibility, elicit scorn, tarnish your brand. That's costly, too.

To create ads that catch the eye, be funny, crafty, outrageous, absolutely. But involve the product or service in the concept. That qualifies your audience. Prevents unwanted clicks. Burnishes your image. Eliminates the wrath.

In some of the strongest banner and social media ads (and for that matter print ads, posters, outdoor billboards, and other forms of advertising), the headline and visual work together to make a cogent statement or captivating teaser.

Here's an ad concept for a website that counsels students and adults pursuing higher education:

Visual: Librarian putting a finger to her lips.

Headline: "Shh! People are researching colleges and careers in our online library. Enter quietly, please"

Sometimes the way you use text can provide visual interest to entice a click. This is for a book about simplifying your life:

Visual: A large black square with tiny white type in the center.

Headline: "Do less."

The following ad for a virtual assistant app targets a specific segment of its market with a problem/solution proposition:

> Visual: Woman screaming into her phone.
>
> Headline: "Dentists lose patients when callers lose patience."

Note, in each of these instances the concept revolves around the product, defining its audience to attract productive clicks.

Considering the distaste for ads on Facebook, LinkedIn, Instagram and other social media, which seem to be inserted in ever greater frequencies, at least try to make them provocative or entertaining. Users are more forgiving of humorous, hip and imaginative.

The opposite approach is to treat social media ads as regular posts. No flair, no hype, just an honest intriguing statement, with or without an image, about your product or service.

This may survive the ad-averse eye and get read, despite the small "Sponsored" or "Promoted" tag in the upper left corner.

44 Print ads and brochures

I put these two items in the same section for a reason. I've always believed the headline concept on a brochure cover should pack as much punch as an ad's. Maybe even more, since there's no guarantee anyone will look inside.

Like online ads, the text and visual synergy should make a strong impression on readers, impelling them to explore further, or, best case, act immediately.

Unfortunately, most brochures settle for a vapid title, a mere company name, or a toothless throw-away line with the expectation you'll flip open the cover and start reading. If only.

Likewise most ads, if you thumb through a magazine, have feeble headlines that fail to capture your eye or interest, looking just like ordinary, predictable, well, *ads*.

Don't merely display product and list features. *Show* people in a dramatic way how it makes their lives better.

Examples of effective headline concepts that struck me when first seen, and have been seared into my memory for many years:

Visual: A crock of steaming, delicious-looking chowder. Headline: "To a clam it's like making the Super Bowl."

Visual: A bottle of Chivas Regal Scotch on the ground, shattered. Headline: "Did you ever see a grown man cry?"

Visual: A muddy-looking cup of joe sitting on a breakfast table. Headline: "Is your coffee grounds for divorce?"

And for Swingline Staplers: Visual: A large image of a paperclip. Headline: "Our only real competition."

(This last was my own, selected for the book *The 100 Greatest Corporate Ads.*)

For brochures, headline/visual concepts should be no less compelling. In fact, any of the above concepts could be adapted for a brochure cover.

What also works is a partial headline on the cover that teases the reader to look inside to the see rest. Here's how a popular collection of travel guides executed this strategy:

> **Cover: "Presenting a Series of Guides So Breathtaking..."**
> **Inside: "It's an Adventure Just Reading Them."**

For the body text of an ad, remember: you're intruding on the reader's perusal of a magazine or newspaper. So keep it as brief, and riveting, as possible.

For brochures, you have more real estate to work with, but be no less frugal with your words, no less crafty in their deployment.

Great way to teach yourself? Read as many ads and brochures as you can get your hands on. See what intrigues, captivates, alarms, delights, inspires, surprises, motivates, and sells *you.*

Then adapt those techniques to your own work.

45 Sales Letters—printed and online

Whether a half-pager you throw in the mail or a 4,000 word webpage, a sales letter can be a formidable promotional tool.

Or it can fall flat on its face, depending on how you write it.

To that point, there's fierce debate on how long a printed sales letter should be. Most writers generally go by this rule:

As long as it takes to procure the sale, capture the lead, prompt a donation, or however you'd like the recipient to respond.

That doesn't help much, which is why many mailings first undergo testing to determine what works best before they're rolled out.

My approach is this. There are few things that can't be sold, or prompt an action, on a single page of 350 words or fewer.

Sales letters of two, three, four, even eight pages or longer can still convert, sure, but they face this sign-of-the-times obstacle:

Anything more than a page risks the recipient putting it aside to read later on. Or more likely, never.

So unless you're selling a complex product or service, or targeting people with a lot of time on their hands, shoot for a one-pager. (You'll save on postage, too.)

For online sales letters the sky's the limit since webpages are bottomless. Though I strongly remind you that breezy, chit-chatty, meandering copy will quickly send visitors to the exit.

Some other tips:

Regardless of length, keep the entire pitch on the same webpage. That way you maintain control, presenting your selling points in the sequence you prefer, rather than your prospects clicking around to other pages, possibly losing them in the process.

Include your call-to-action link or phone number periodically throughout to accommodate those sold early on, or who haven't time to finish reading, on the chance they'll take the bait before departing.

Creatively formatting an online letter, especially a lengthy one, is vital to maintaining interest. Spice it up with images, charts, sidebars, testimonials, and other devices if you can.

Keep sentences and paragraphs short with ample space in between to make them more inviting to read.

Vary the text by using bold, italics, underlines, indents, and other font attributes. Insert frequent section headings.

As to the content of your letter, whether printed or online, try adhering to the advice for clarity, brevity and engagement dispensed in Part One.

Here's an example of a single-page sales letter I wrote that aided in the successful launch of the business magazine *Fast Company:*

> Get your hands on a FREE issue of
> FAST COMPANY. You'll never let go.

Dear Business Professional:

Get out the highlighter, the scissors, the notepad, the routing envelopes.

Your free issue of *Fast Company* is just a reply card away! *Fast Company* is unlike any business publication you've ever known. As revolutionary as the new face of business it reports on.

Don't expect a magazine that lulls you to sleep on the train. Or merely offers you "perspective."

This is front burner stuff all the way. Intelligence you can act on, pass along and profit from.

Today.

Fast Company attracts a special kind of reader. One who isn't content just to know what's happening...but *makes* things happen. Sound like someone you know?

One caveat. Don't lend your free issue to anyone. You'll

never get it back.

This is crucial: if you value *Fast Company*, subscribe to *Fast Company*. That way, you're assured of getting every issue. (It flies off the newsstands.)

We're not talking big bucks here. Just $14.95 for a year— a savings of 37% off the cover price.

Now I'll shut up. Let the magazine speak. Just be sure to send the enclosed Free Trial Issue Request in the postage-paid envelope to receive your free copy.

Then roll up your sleeves. And get to work.

Sincerely,

WHITE PAPERS

46 Marketing's missing in action

You've got a knockout website. Eye-catching ads. Explosive email blasts. A lively social media presence.

But where are your white papers? Do you even know what a white paper is? Better find out.

A white paper should be an essential component of your marketing mix. Without it you're just a lot of hype, with nothing that sets you apart as an expert in your field.

Your white paper can be an objective report, article, guide, or blog post on a particular aspect of your business or industry. The operative word is here "objective."

This is not advertising. It should be honest, factual and (this is where many white papers fall short) *engaging*. It informs your audience in a way no advertising can. Knowledge and advice they can rely on to make sound purchasing decisions.

White papers foster a strong and trustworthy relationship with your clientele. They establish you as a thought leader in your industry and boost the credibility of your products and services.

47 White papers are all-purpose, too.

Many trade magazines publish white papers (if they're not overtly self-promoting) as articles—an invaluable source of free publicity and an explicit endorsement of your expertise.

Of course, you'll want to feature the white paper on your website. And include a link to it, with a brief description of its contents, in your emails, on social media, and in other correspondence.

Or send out a press release announcing its publication, making it an event in itself.

White papers also make great handouts at trade shows, on sales calls, or in press kits. Or throw them in an envelope and snail-mail to a list of your prime prospects and customers. You see the kind of legs white papers can have.

48 Don't draw a blank when it comes to white papers

So now that you know what they are, what they do and ways to disseminate them...how do you write them?

Pick an aspect of your business to cover. Industry trends, product or service innovations, regulatory changes, advanced production methods, new distribution channels. The options are endless.

Do your research. As you dig, you'll get ideas. Canvass trade magazines that specialize in your business to see what the hot topics are. Note how they handle them journalistically.

Keep in mind what you learned earlier in this book. No fluff. No filler. No waltzing around your subject. Get to the point. Publications don't have space, nor readers time, to waste.

To give your white paper credibility, use statistics from reliable sources, quotes from industry experts. Back them up with attributions and footnotes.

Make white papers an integral, recurring part of your marketing plan. They will pay for themselves many times over by enhancing your brand image and business integrity.

OFFICE COMMUNICATIONS

49 Great place to polish your skills

The bulk of anyone's business writing, no surprise, consists of emails, reports, texts, work orders, briefing docs, project updates—you know, the grunt stuff.

As a daily recipient of such things, I'm appalled at how the level of professionalism in everyday business communications has tanked.

Not just flagrant typos, omitted words, bad grammar, poor usage, and the like. There's plenty of that.

What galls most is the inability of people to clearly express themselves, the failure to reread what they've written to be sure it's understandable, the questions their writing leaves unanswered, the confusion caused by statements that can be construed in more than one way.

I know, everyone's busy. But making the effort to write clearly and accurately will save time, boost productivity and minimize frustration *on all sides* in the long run.

And guess what? It makes you look polished, professional, on top of your game. Ripe for advancement. Who doesn't want that?

Take the time to get it right. And assure recipients it's not their fault if something isn't clear: "Please let me know if anything doesn't make sense. I'm happy to clarify."

One more thing. An epidemic of exclamation-pointitis is raging throughout the business world. With no cure in sight.

If that's how you and your personal contacts like to dialogue, fine.

But in business? It comes off like a hyperactive puppy unable to contain itself. This is not the image of experience and maturity you want to project. Is it?

Here's an actual email I received from a recruiter:

> Hi Jerry!!
>
> Do you know any senior branding copywriters with experience at a branding agency???
>
> Let us know or forward this email to your friends and colleges! [sic]
>
> Thanks!!!
>
> Best wishes!

I was tempted to reply: No! I don't! Sorry!

PART THREE IF I'VE LEARNED ANYTHING...

Over decades of incredible change, certain aspects of writing have, at least for me, never changed. I share a few of them here in the hope of sparing you the time and occasional anguish of learning the hard way.

50 Edit, edit, edit

No grumbling, now. What would you rather do: subject your work to rigorous self-editing or have someone do it for you? Especially if you love what you've done. Especially if the one editing your baby hasn't a clue.

You've got help in this area. Time. It's as potent an editor as there is. Opt for shorter, spaced-out writing sessions rather than long, slap-it-together marathons. (Do other stuff in between.)

Let the work marinate a few hours, or overnight (the subconscious will work on it while you sleep).

When you come back to it, you'll immediately see places where you can express something better. Less convolutedly. More concisely.

Doubt that? Read things you wrote a few months or even years ago you thought you nailed. If you're like me, you'll have a few cringeworthy moments.

I've found the more I edit something the less others will tamper with it. Good, tight writing builds a wall of protection around itself. It doesn't have many openings for someone to pry their way in and muck things up. On the other hand...

51 Take honest suggestions seriously

Don't get ruffled when someone who's required to review your work before it goes out suggests a few edits. I've found most people usually have valid points to make.

Their comments will be factual, not style-based, and your work will be better for it. Business communication isn't fine art. So don't be crushed when a team member chimes in. It's part of the process. Yet...

52 Beware the chronic noodler

If you do encounter someone (in my case, often a low-level functionary on the client side exerting petty power) who's tearing brilliantly written copy apart, go on offense.

That means politely challenging each change they're trying to inflict. Make them defend their nitpicking. They'll soon run out of rationales, grow weary, get the message.

If you strongly disagree with an edit, ignore it in the next draft. Odds are they won't even remember it.

If all this doesn't work, it's time to exercise the nuclear option. Yup. You may think it's risky, but it's rarely failed me:

Sigh resignedly, apologize and declare you'll just have to rewrite the entire project from the beginning. Horrified they'll be causing unnecessary delays, fearful of possible blowback from superiors, their picayune obstinacy exposed, they'll back off.

53 Proof, proof, proof

There's a mistake in that report. Oh yeah, and probably more than one. It's up to you to find them. Make a game of it. Read over the work at a normal pace. Then again, slowly, checking each word and punctuation. You'll be surprised what you missed.

You might think a few mistakes are okay since everyone else is making them. Like the amount of allowable bacteria in ice cream. I would scrap that notion.

Know this. Every error in your writing, cumulatively over time, chips away at the image of conscientiousness, credibility and competency you project.

Business associates, clients, customers, suppliers are not your social media buddies. Letting your professional guard down when communicating with them may come back to bite you.

Clean up that document. Eradicate those errors. Proof, proof, proof.

54 Writer's block? *What* writer's block?

I, like every scribe on the planet, am prone to periodic bouts of writer's block. It's taken years to figure out how to conquer it, so here's what works for me.

To get the juices flowing, I take my cue from artists. Do they sit there staring at a blank canvas? Heck no. They start sketching, and sketching, roughly, letting ideas spew out, then revising them, refining them, until something more definitive takes shape.

Do that with your writing. Roughly write down anything that comes to mind, *anything*, remotely related to your task. Add other thoughts as they occur. Reserve judgment. It may be ugly, but hey, you've got something.

Now, go have a cup of coffee, take a walk, a nap, whatever. When you return, see where you can improve on it. Repeat as directed.

At some point, the big picture will start to materialize. Your path will begin to lay out before you. Then, bingo!, a brilliant opening will present itself. You're off to the races.

55 When it's good, you know it. Ditto, bad

If we're brutally honest, we'll admit to ourselves when our writing has an uncomfortable odor emanating from it. Or it's struggling to stand on wobbly legs. Or it just isn't measuring up.

My rule is this. If you have even an inkling that what you wrote might not be clear, it's not.

If you sense certain phrasing may not be strong enough, it isn't.

If you feel the whole thing is flat, that it just doesn't have the zing you were striving for, you're right.

Trust your instincts. Always ask yourself: "Can I say this in a more provocative, sensitive, humorous, dramatic, factual, emotional, succinct, or emphatic way?"

The answer is usually yes, you can. So get to it. Never send out anything you're not totally happy with.

56 Revisit your past work periodically

You may have heard of TV and movie actors who never watch their own performances because they hate what they see: glaring moments they regret they could have done better.

Understandable, but for writers I believe it's necessary. Looking back at things you've written in the past can be an instructive, albeit sometimes humbling, experience.

Regardless if the effort was good, middling or awful, mistakes you made, opportunities you missed will jump out at you, not having benefited from the knowledge and wisdom you've gained since.

Revisit work when enough distance has crept in to see it as others do. You'll learn a lot and become a better communicator.

Finally:

57 Be a proponent of breakthrough business communication

Business blather is so deeply entrenched in the corporate ethos, it may take a long time to knock it off its faux pedestal.

But that will make your work stand out all the more, if you strive to create innovative, engrossing, concise written and spoken communications more attuned to the way we live and work today.

Whether writing is incidental to your occupation, a large part of it, or you're making a career out of it, I hope this book and its precepts will serve as a launching pad to soar above the morass of pretentious babble and deliver the impact you seek.

If so, kindly recommend it to your colleagues and friends.

I welcome your comments and suggestions. Please email me at: jerrymct321@gmail.com

Enjoy the rewards of inspired authorship!

ABOUT THE AUTHOR

Jerry McTigue is a professional business writer, copywriter, journalist, author, and scriptwriter with decades of experience crafting every kind of business communication imaginable.

He is the author of seven books that have been featured on hundreds of radio and TV shows, and numerous articles and essays that have appeared in major city newspapers and national magazines.

His copywriting prowess has earned him the coveted CLIO and ANDY awards for advertising excellence.

He is a member of the American Society of Journalists and Authors (ASJA) and a resident of New York City.

"The most valuable of all talents is that of never using two words when one will do."

—Thomas Jefferson